Saint-Paul-de-Mausole

Matt Haw

Saint-Paul-de-Mausole

Copyright Matt Haw, 2014

The right of Matt Haw to be identified as the author of this work has been asserted in accordance with the Copyright, Designs and Patents Act 1988.

ISBN – 13: 978-1-904551-93-5

A CIP record for this title is available from the British Library.

Published by tall-lighthouse press.

Acknowledgements

Acknowledgements are due to the editors of *Long Poem Magazine* and *The London Magazine* in which some of these poems first appeared. Acknowledgements and gratitude are also due to the Arts and Humanities Research Council and the Eric Gregory Trust for funding and prize money. My thanks go to Helena Nelson for her diligent reading and to Adam Barrett and April McIntyre for love and unerring faith.

Saint-Paul-de-Mausole is dedicated to Tim Liardet, Carrie Etter, the staff and poetry students of Bath Spa University's Creative Writing MA programme 2011/2012.

Saint-Paul-de-Mausole

"Sometimes moods of indescribable anguish, sometimes moments when the veil of time and fatality of circumstances seemed to be torn apart for an instant."

Vincent van Gogh

Notes on the Case History
of a Monothematic Delusion

I will concern myself with Mr Alain Gillo, a patient of particular interest. Born in Norfolk in 1982, in late adolescence he began to experience prolonged bouts of chronic depression. After graduating from the Norwich School of Art and Design, he took up a job as a printmaker in the city but suffered a complete breakdown at the age of twenty-five, shortly after sustaining a savage and unprovoked attack.

At the time of his attack, Mr Gillo was entering a most acute and profound depressive episode. I have no doubt that the physical trauma of the attack was a catalyst in the decline of his mental health. He stopped going to work and the relationship with his long term partner deteriorated. He was compelled to go and stay with his parents in order to recuperate. By the time he was brought to my attention he had become delusional and quite paranoid, convinced that his now ex-partner had been involved, in some tortuous capacity, in the attack. Most startling though was the patient's neurosis, which had manifested itself as an obsessive, psychotic relationship with the artist Vincent van Gogh.

Preoccupied with perceived parallels observed between himself and van Gogh, Mr Gillo claimed that, in his reflection, he saw the artist's face in place of his own. He showed me a number of manipulated photographs and self-portraits of how he saw himself, these works appearing as pastiches of van Gogh's distinct style of portraiture. Mr Gillo was indeed of similar appearance to van Gogh and was possessed of a certain intensity of character similar to the emotional sensitivity for which van Gogh is renowned. As the patient's obsession deepened he confided to me that he'd tried to contact the dead painter though a homemade Ouija board, that, in sleep, he was plagued by vivid dreams of the asylum where van Gogh had been incarcerated towards the end of his life.

The patient's dreams of the asylum varied; at times he was able to recount whole vignettes of action and dialogue. I have gathered that he occupied certain points of view: as a spectre, haunting the corridors of the old monastery; as minor characters, an orderly, medical intern or other employee of the asylum who engaged in superficial interactions with the artist.

During one session, Mr Gillo recounted a dream in which he was standing at the entrance to the asylum. "The iron gates", he said, "opened onto a rough driveway that unwound towards the building through a garden. It was dusk and the windows of the asylum were unlit. In darkness under the trees, a shadowy figure prowled between the trunks."

– Dr S.K. Zarahbi. London, 2012

"Tall trees stand out against a yellow evening sky crossed with purple, yielding to pink and green higher up. The nearest pine has been struck by lightning and sawn off, however one branch still juts up into the air and sends down a rain of dark green needles…"

Letter from Vincent van Gogh to Emile Bernard, 20th November 1889

1

Monologue I

Above the asylum the sky is a slick
of spilt milk, of broken-glass stars.
Across the chimney stacks of Saint-Rémy,
the wind moves in laboured breaths.

Tonight, that same wind squalls
round this little suburban garden,
lifting the gate in the alley from its latch,
flinging umber leaves in savage arabesques.

It comes alive where it finds the spaces
between clothing and skin, comes alive
in the hairs on the nape of my neck.

It's as if you leant one cheek
against the still wet canvas of the world
and sighed – and sighed – and sighed.

Hôtel-Dieu-Saint-Espirit

You remembered nothing of the attack,

nothing of the ruck of Gendarme

who braced against your punches and scissor-

kicks, against the hooked fish of your body,

who unhanded you to the isolation cell

where, at last, you were Torquato Tasso

just as Delacroix thought of him:

a heap of skin and straightjacket

left to subdue your own torso.

Alone with the swung drum of your heart,

you amused yourself with the eyes

of the peepshow actors breaking character

to stare back through the Judas hole

into the eyes of the man who observed them.

The Statement

The fist, caught on my chin,

ploughs a furrow in the loam

of my face. It sends me palming

the asphalt, spitting a mouthful

of broken teeth. Nickel-tang

on the tongue, lick of blood on the cheek.

My fingers and crushed fingernails

hug my knees like things long-lost.

The Nike-clad heels hammer down,

hammer down and hammer down.

Down here, where the world turns

to leaf mould and dog shit, I turn to road kill,

a heap of dead fox, in a jaggy pelt

one size too small for its bones.

What weight does a fist contain?

It's not measured in kilos or tons but still

I might weigh the whole world

by the poundage of flesh brought down

on my brow, again and again, a sovereign

to break my skin. Our pact of harm.

Think of a crush of men,

the way a dozen of them can be fused

by violence, and the ferocity

of twenty-four feet, twenty-four fists.

At the drain cover where glass

puddled and sparked, *why*

blood-bubbled at my lips

but would not commit itself to the word.

The Asylum

> "Some patients are very seriously ill and you
> continually hear terrible cries and howls like
> beasts in a menagerie…. Someone here has
> been shouting and talking like me."
>
> Letter from Vincent van Gogh to Emile
> Bernard, 22nd May 1889

When calmed, this drunkship of exiles
played at Dostoyevsky or held
conversations with half-heard echoes.
In the asylum Saint-Paul-de-Mausole
– that house of the dead – the doctors
prescribed to the men of the menagerie
draughts and boules and lethargy.

Confined to your room, you spent time
getting used to your changed reflection.
You calmed yourself with an infinitude
of small things: a kept cicada shell,

a blade of grass, a pine cone, with views

of cypress trees and wheat fields.

With the touch of brush to canvas.

*

There were bowls of chick peas

and haricot beans gone musty

with the roach infestation

but what hunger you had was lost

to a belly full of soil and turpentine.

In your room your work gorged

on canvas and paint to balance

your lack of appetite.

In this place there are those who howl

and those who must endure the howling.

You steeled yourself with alcohol,

with nicotine, with caffeine

and a crush of camphor under the pillow.

Charms against the cold house.

Midnight in A&E

I breathe disinfectant. Formaldehyde.
I bleed into gauze an impressionist's
bouquet of all the red flowers I know.

There are others with me, concussives
and paralytics, each consumed
by self-pity, each snow-blinded

by the white-on-white, the strip-lighting.
We wait our turn to be led to the ward
and sutured by a nurse with seen-it-before eyes.

Was I the only one to see you, tacked
to the wall, to notice the skinny-lipped
half-smirk of *Self-Portrait, September 1889*?

You poster boy for chronic depression.
You patron saint of hospital corridors.

Potassium Bromide

Sedative. Anticonvulsant. The name conjures
images of chemical snow, corked phials
ranked and labelled in a mahogany box.
Yes, it was as barbarous as it sounds.
The compound is used in photographic developer
and better suited, I'm told, as a curative for beasts.
Nonetheless, the doctors, in white coats
and pince-nez, seasoned your water
and left you to the pharmaceutical salts
dissolving across your tongue. You quaked
with the unintended side-effects of ataxia,
and delirium. Like the men
who passed their barks, as one voice,
through the halls of the asylum.

'This Train Will Stop At Brundall, Cantley, Reedham'

The stopping train brought me home,

a single carriage beam of light

across the midnight marshes and fen,

empty for driver and me.

I tried to recall my parents' house.

The garden with its broken gate.

Scratches of rain on the kitchen window.

The few plants I knew by name;

I no longer recognised the things

which no longer recognised me.

On the platform I watched the train

pull away and vanish into darkness

on tracks rimed with frost. The engine

that must have been going somewhere.

Diagnosing a Dead Man

Any attempt at diagnosis
is a waste of time. As if an answer to *you*
could be found in *Anatomies of Melancholy*
or the *DSM*. Tell me, Vincent,

tell me how you bit down
on your tongue until your molars
touched like two halves of a scabulous pearl.
You curled back a plum-flesh lip,

snarled and seethed at the universe
through clenched teeth. You spat
rosaries of saliva and blood.

How you sated an unthinkable hunger
with soil and paint.
        With lamp oil.
                With turpentine.

Changeling

What made it back to my parents' house,
back through the sleet and darkness
to the door of that suburban detached?
I was not their son.
More a feral child who dripped blood
on the front step. Whose tongue could utter
only grunts. Whose lips were fat with bruise
and scrunched to the right.
I didn't even recognise my own image
in the door glass. I was confronted instead
by your face. Then the porch lamp
threw out its light and mother
had to see son in the creature.

The Water Glass

Strange to think of snow that far south,

of a cold that barbs the air,

shanking breaths in the larynx.

Did the blizzard settle in the bare

orchards and vineyards? The sky

a tangle of snow and starlight. Too much.

Think of the sick man's

mind. Of the chemical imbalance

which sets molecules misfiring

in the synapses, spinning out an aura

across the vision, chrome-bright shapes.

Of the sweat and lockjaw.

Of the flail that brought a glass

slipping from the window sill.

*

Something was broken. Imagine the limb-spasm
and the physics of the falling glass.
Imagine it in slow-mo, shedding globs

of water, measuring the time it takes
for lightning to flash in the synaptic
chasms. Was it light enough to absorb

the shock of the terracotta?
Only the dead know such things. Perhaps
the impact sent a delta of hairline cracks

across its surface before the glass exploded out
into the world. Perhaps water shuddered,
held itself for a moment. When the deluge

came down on the tiles, the snuff
of glass you rolled in was starlike.

Dream I

Don't believe for a moment we never met.
In dreams I am an intern pacing the old asylum,
drawn to one of perhaps a hundred doors.
I find you inside slumped on your bed,
hauled up from the isolation cell.

Blood runs where the looped bandage
curls over your ear like rank hair.
Sitting by your bed, I unwind
the yellowed gauze. Such a wound
defines a man and I confess

I liked to look at what remained of the ear.
I took my time sponging it clean.

When I woke I thought it was
your blood scabbing my fingernails.

The Sickroom

Think of my room as the space
on the other side of a mirror.
It is gloomy. Only twilight dares
the journey through the glass.

I imagine you'd feel right at home
with these spartan furnishings:
single bed, wicker chair, the lamp
left on in hope – a storm lantern

to coax you out of the dark.
Perhaps you'll skulk in
through the window. Take a seat
on the chair. That's right. Now

in my private Saint-Paul-de-Mausole,
we can talk. We can compare wounds.

Ghost Caduceus

Closer and closer our dog-dance draws us

until your body hair is snagging my own.

I think I can number the pores on your nose.

We circle each other, a taut-line of flesh.

Your chin on my neck, my calf on your shin.

Impossible to unpick, we have become

a time-lapse portrait of a ballerina

whose pirouette left tangled

limb with limb, vertebrae with rib.

Each movement works to lash us tighter,

mounting pressure on sacrum, clavicle, sternum

until the last breathing space left between us,

at armpit, groin, throat and lung, closes up.

Nothing but blue to be wrung from our union.

No bindings, just muscle, bone and sinew.

I am halfway dressed in a costume of you,

your arms in my sleeve,

my neck in your collar.

Our warped physiques press:

navel, nipple, heel blister, lumbar tattoo.

They divide between us the features

distinguishing one from the other:

the birthmarks down my stomach,

your cheek freckles, your nose freckles.

How else can I comprehend your tongue

in my mouth, your breath in my throat?

Or the way our eyes simultaneously look

square into and out of each other?

Séance

Consider the imperatives of talking to a ghost,
how remote your voice would sound,
wax cylinder faint. You would speak
a fractured English, in breaths
that wouldn't fog a mirror.

I rigged a make-shift Ouija board,
placed my fingers to a bled shot glass
and waited.
               Capricious in death,
you'd as likely spit in my face as lay
a hand on my shoulder. I was tense,
ready for the cold draught, the smell
of saltpetre, coffee, pipe smoke.
But the glass stayed calm, leaking
its dregs. I lost my nerve.

Monologue II

I was sick as a dog. That much I knew.
Sickness was in my stomach. I retched

on my fingers. Sickness was in my head.

I tried to smash it out against the toilet bowl.

Sickness was in my blood. I opened my veins,
tried to bleed sickness from me. Sickness
was in my fingers and toes. I peeled
off each nail: *she loves me, she loves me not.*
Sickness was in my groin. I was impotent
and couldn't piss. Finally

I tried to ignore sickness. My lead tongue.

My aching balls. But the door was locked.
The curtains had drawn themselves.
The house bred unfathomable silences.

Dream II

Where the choppy wheat tilts
bleached fields to the sun,
you fasten down your easel
with ropes. With pig-iron nails,

half a metre long, you anchor yourself
to the earth against the mistral
that would make a jib of your paintings,
lift you skyward. Will your improvised

attachments hold back the energy of flight?
The air has already claimed your famous
straw hat and is hungry for more.

How long before the wind sets
the great cabbage whites of your canvases
scatter-flapping across the field?

Amy

She was gorgeous in her army-surplus

greatcoat, standing at my door,

framed by a darkness perforated

with snow and streetlight.

In my room, she guided unscrupulous hands

to the coarse wool lapels, had me pull them

open like the twenty-fourth door

of an advent calendar. Are you ready

for your close-up, darling?

She wore knee-high boots, French-cuts,

her breasts, cinnamon-freckled and cupped

in their bra, her lips a red smudge,

mascara blurring lugubrious eyes.

　　　Had our roles been switched, Vincent,

　　　she'd have been the whore who got my ear

*

All I know of love I've lifted
from hearsay and films. So pity the girl
who gave her heart to a boy half imagined,
half fraud. In short, a boy *bound*

to let her down. My silence
drew her back. In that self-same greatcoat
she hammered at my door,
her mouth crowded out with all the *cunts*

and *fuck-yous* her tongue would allow.
Was it she who picked me out that night?
I think of her, shadow in a passenger seat,

pouting into her mirror. Her lipstick drawn
across a mouth full with envy. From the Latin:
invidere – to regard maliciously.

The First Law of Gossip

Two constables, bald, pink-faced,
identical in their stab-vests
and beetle-black boots, came to take
my statement. They wanted to know

exactly where and when the attack happened.
They asked me why. I couldn't answer.
Grunting they concluded their report.
In the wake of their custodial visit

there was mud and slush tracked onto
the hall carpet and the static
of rumour charged by silence.

But you know how details get distorted
in the telling and the retelling. Until no one
can be sure what really happened.

Dream III

The olive grove was freckled
with sunlight. At midday
even the cicadas were silent.
The heat could send you mad.

I see you out there, smudged
by mirage. Your lips blistered
as if breath could scorch flesh.

What whim compelled you to lift
to your mouth your brush?
The bristles loaded with clods
of burnt sienna, cerulean,

carmine and emerald green.
To stain your teeth with a froth
of mango, of pomegranate, of fig.

Self-Portrait as Vincent van Gogh I

First there was a skull. Off white, grinning

like an idiot under its empty eye sockets.

Skull spawned a scowl, two bruise-heavy lips.

Scowl spawned a muzzle prickled with hair,

a nose that oozed red. Muzzle spawned

cheeks, a clenched-fist brow, a mane

of hair close-shaved here and there for stitches.

The face spawned two heterochromic eyes:

one green eye, one blue eye, and a cut-throat

razor blade to split itself down the middle

bisecting the brow and nose and lips

like two halves of a rotting peach.

And one half of it was mine, Vincent,

And the other half was yours.

Self-Portrait as Vincent van Gogh II

This is my body's

ruinous topography: knapped flint

teeth, scabbed knuckles,

an avalanche of flesh

plumblue with the atolls

of bootmarks. This is my nose.

This is my right eye buried

under lids swelled inch thick.

A penumbra of you is cast

across this self-portrait

in the bathroom mirror;

across the part of me

that, after the attack,

made it back to my body.

Self-Portrait as Vincent van Gogh III

At what juncture was I sculpted
in your image? When were the primary hues
of brutality worked so deep in my skin?

I remember the Sanskrit of sleet thumbing blood
from my face, the plunge of jet engines –
low, visceral – on the runway approach.

The words of the man who found me:
like something out of a film noir. A chiaroscuro shot,
sodium-lit, the firmament almost within reach,

and centre frame a man, yes, I think it's a man,
though pared-back to a shadow feeding the verge
and poplars of Calvary Street. And then,

the narrator's hard-boiled voice kicks in
to introduce himself - at this point, dead.

Self-Portrait as Vincent van Gogh **IV**

The house floods across the lawn,

in window and porch light. From here,

pressed close to the window glass,

I can detect the smell of snow.

This tête-à-tête with the outside

is my latest attempt to speak with your ghost.

Sure enough, a bruise bleeds into the glass,

a half-reflection I almost mistake

for your self-portrait – as if all glass

remembers your image. This furtive

mock-up of myself is quiet. The mouth

takes its time around a sigh. The eyes

are smudged into sockets that stare,

stare as if I am trying to outstare you.

The Garden on a December Afternoon

I am drawn to the end of the garden,

stepping beyond the pools of leaves

squared by the light the kitchen windows

hurl across the lawn. Here the grass

is sweet with moss and windfall

and I cradle the butt of a cigarette

against the sleet. The easy winter

darkness seems to strum the nerves.

I become aware of the vast distances

my lungs suck in, twilight

as a breathable thing. I almost expect

to find you here. Sprawled out

in the carpet ivy, painting

the drew as it tenses to a frost.

Dream IV

The men of the asylum declare themselves
with footsteps, growls and slammed doors.

All the usual trickery – as if being ghosts
has robbed them of imagination. They vanish

round corners, leading me through the house of corridors.
This milieu rendered in a single hue – call it ghost

or dream-blue – the rest of the spectrum elsewhere.
You took it with you when you left

with the other traces of your life: the initials
you scored in the bed frame, the walls;

the shadows of paint you spilt across the floor.
In the places where the world requisitions

its artists and madmen, I must be content

with talking to myself.

The Visitor

What woke me the night I saw you?

Was it the storm that slapped against the house

and spun gibberish through the telegraph wires?

Was it the hypnic jerk that heaved me back

to my body? To a room distorted

by the orange darkness of cul-de-sac night.

I was a frightened child again.

                    I glimpsed you from my window

through a static of snow, walking

the path toward the house. You brought

a wind which bent itself around itself

in vast whorls, congealed with the pressure of the air.

Which exhaled and inhaled, exhaled and inhaled

as though something was trying to speak.